Yes! I Can Make A Difference

Copyright © 2008 Go MAD Ltd
The rights of Go MAD Ltd to be identified as the author of this work have been asserted in accordance with the Copyright, Designs and Patents Act 1988.

First published in Great Britain in 1999 by:
Go MAD Books
Pocket Gate Farm
Off Breakback Road
Woodhouse Eaves
Leicestershire
LE12 8RS

All rights reserved. No part of this publication may be reproduced, stored in a retrieval system, or transmitted in any form or by any means without the prior written consent of the publisher.

ISBN 0-9543292-9-5

British Library Cataloguing in Publication Data.
A catalogue record for this book is available from the British Library.

Printed and bound in Great Britain by
Hudson & Pearson Ltd
Burnley

Go MAD® is a registered trademark

Introduction

"If I had an hour to solve a problem and my life depended on the solution, I would spend the first 55 minutes determining the proper question to ask, for once I know the proper question, I could solve the problem in less than 5 minutes."
Albert Einstein

If asking a great question is so important, why don't most people invest more time and effort in crafting and designing them? A well crafted, high quality, question designed to help yourself or others can stop a person in their tracks – often accompanied by an initial statement such as: "Wow. Good question!" – as their thinking is taken to a new level or a more helpful place.

So what questions will be the most helpful for you to consider in order to move forward, find solutions and make a difference? Are you able to ask yourself the helpful questions or would you like some help with your thinking?

Questions are just one element of our thinking – albeit the easiest to influence. When we think we also talk inwardly to ourself in the form of statements, often commenting on ourself, our abilities, our perception of others and the current situation. The phraseology and vocal tone of these statements will either help or hinder our ability to achieve results. Likewise the memories we recall and the future we imagine will also influence the actions we take and the results we achieve.

A solution focused approach to thinking

I realised, as a result of much research and learning, that if I maintained my helpful thoughts and replaced my hindering thoughts with ones that were more helpful, this would be more likely to help me achieve greater results. So, by asking better quality questions, talking to myself in a helpful way, recalling useful things from the past and focusing on the future I desired, I could significantly improve my probability of success. A solution focused approach to thinking would inevitably lead me to take different actions and hence achieve different results.

Thinking ⟶ Actions ⟶ Results
(helpful or hindering?)

The challenge is to stop and think before jumping straight into taking action.

A bit about the Go M.A.D.® research

In 1997 I became fascinated by the whole subject of achievement and 'Making A Difference' (MAD). So over 14 months I led a major research study (over 4000 hours) to identify the key success principles that people naturally apply when making a difference and achieving success. In essence, I pieced together the 'D.N.A.' pattern of how to make a measurable difference.

This resulted in the development of the Go MAD (Make A Difference) Framework comprising 7 interlinked key success principles. This can be applied as a thinking system to help individuals, teams and organisations question, decide, act and measure the differences they are seeking to make.

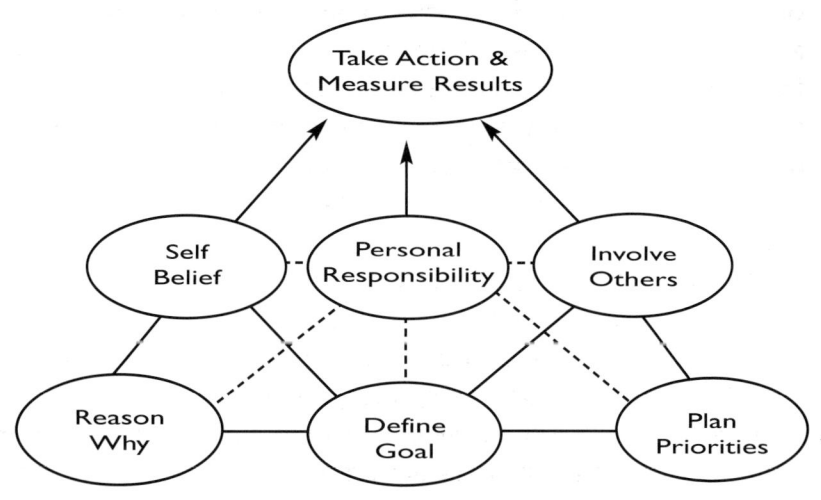

```
                Take Action &
                Measure Results

    Self        Personal         Involve
    Belief      Responsibility   Others

    Reason      Define           Plan
    Why         Goal             Priorities
```

The Go MAD® Framework

Taking Einstein's advice about spending quality time designing quality questions, we can consider:
- What is my clearly defined goal?
- How strong is my motivation? (Reason Why)
- How can I maintain or build my level of confidence? (Self Belief)
- What are the possible tasks, resources, reasons for involving others, risks, assumptions, obstacles and ways to overcome them?
- Who could I involve and how do I gain their buy-in?
- How much time will I set aside for my important priorities?
- How much personal responsibility am I willing to take?
- What actions will I take?
- When and how will I measure my results?

Once these key success principles and the relationships between them are clearly understood, and the relevant skills are developed, then Go MAD can be applied as a solution focused thinking system to improve the probability of achieving results.

How solution focused is your thinking system?
Thinking about your thinking and the thinking of others in your organisation. In fact, how many thinking systems are there in your organisation? (Clue: How many people are there?) How many are problem focused/hindering rather than solution focused/helpful? Now imagine, what if there was a shared thinking system, with a practical toolkit for everyone to use – a framework based on key success principles that everyone could apply? Do you think it might improve the probability of success?

Go MAD Thinking Applications
The Go MAD Framework is being applied by hundreds of thousands of people in over 30 countries. Most use it to increase their personal effectiveness; many apply it as a coaching framework to help others think in a solution focused way; some use it as a shared thinking system within their team, whilst others

have transformed their organisation by embedding it in their culture.

The Go MAD team work worldwide designing a range of management, leadership and business improvement programmes. Underpinning each of these is the Go MAD Framework and a toolkit of solution focused techniques and thinking skills which, when applied, as a shared thinking system ensures measurable results are achieved.

So, what now?
You can choose to fill this book with personal thoughts, use it as a personal journal, use it to capture notes from the development programme you might now be attending, use the quotations for inspiration or take time to answer the 119 questions. The choice is yours. Think, take action and make a difference.

Andy Gilbert

"The purpose of our lives is to be happy."
The Fourteenth Dalai Lama

Q: What do you want to write this book about?

"Success lies in doing not what others consider to be great, but what you consider to be right."
John Henry Gray

Q: What step can I take today to move towards what I want?

"In the middle of difficulty lies opportunity."
Albert Einstein

Q: What impact do I want to make?

"Neither fire nor wind, birth nor death
can erase our good deeds."
Buddha

Q: What changes have I been avoiding?

"There is nothing permanent except change."
Heraclitus

Q: What attributes do I possess?

"We are what we repeatedly do."
Aristotle

Q: How clear is my focus on the specific difference I want to make?

"Words may show a man's wit, but actions his meaning."
Benjamin Franklin

13

Q: What could I possibly imagine in terms of my success?

"Success is for you, not others, to define."
Brian Weltgred

Q: How strong is my desire?

"Kites rise highest against the wind – not with it."
Winston Churchill

Q: What makes me happy?

"Waste no tears over the griefs of yesterday."
Euripides

16

Q: What is the source of my reason for wanting to make a difference?

"If I have the belief that I can do it, I shall surely acquire the capacity to do it even if I may not have it at the beginning."
Mahatma Gandhi

Q: How do I define success?

"Well done is better than well said."
Benjamin Franklin

Q: What gives me the greatest satisfaction?

""When you possess a passion or strong enough reason why, no-one else has to motviate you to make a difference."
Warren Digbelt

Q: How would I like others to describe me?

"The smallest difference is a million times better than indifference."
Kathryn Roberts

20

Q: What are my priorities?

"Life shrinks or expands in proportion to one's own courage."
Anais Nin

Q: What do I like about myself?

"Nothing happens unless first a dream."
Carl Sandburg

22

Q: Who do I enjoy spending time with?

"Accept what you cannot change;
change what you cannot accept."
Andy Gilbert

Q: Who can I praise or encourage today?

"Behaviour breeds behaviour –
if you make a difference others will follow."
Ken Hudson

24

Q: What positive statement can I make about myself?

"I believe in life after birth."
Maxie Dunham

Q: Whose opinions do I respect and trust?

"If only we could stop saying 'if only'."
Ian Chakravorty

Q: When will I start taking action?

"Imagination rules the world."
Napoleon

Q: How will I measure my progress?

"The time left is all we have got. It makes sense therefore to use it on the things we have prioritised as most important in our lives."
Greta W. Brindle

Q: What am I going to do next?

"You see things and say 'why?'
But I dream things that never were and say 'why not?'"
George Bernard Shaw

Q: How will I thank others for helping me?

"A man has to live with himself, and he should see to it that he always has good company."
Charles Hughes

Q: What legacy will I leave?

"Your attitude is more important than your intellect."
Bridget Walner

Q: How will I take greater personal responsibility for making it happen?

"Work to become, not to acquire."
Elbert Hubbard

Q: What makes life worth living?

"I will act as if what I do makes a difference."
William James

Q: How will I plan more effective use of my time?

"Do what you can with what you have, where you are."
Theodore Roosevelt

Q: What am I looking forward to?

"Make a difference – tell someone how special they are."
Gale Witts

Q: How much time do I spend doing the things I really want to do?

"It is in our choices Harry, that we show what we truly are, far more than our abilities."
Professor Dumbledore to Harry Potter

36

Q: What is the quality of my working relationship with Colleagues?

"Nurture your minds with great thoughts.
To believe in the heroic makes heroes."
Benjamin Disraeli

Q: What makes me laugh?

"You can measure the strength of a desire by the obstacles it is capable of overcoming."
W. Timothy Galloway

Q: What is my most empowering belief about my abilities?

"The most important relationship you will ever have is the relationship you have with yourself."
Dr. Wang Breet Li

Q: What is my internal voice telling me to make a difference about?

"The focused mind can pierce through stone."
Japanese saying

40

Q: How much money do I need?

"Be ready to change because change will happen."
Lt. Barnie Grewd

Q: How could I possibly create the right environment?

"You get what your mind predominantly focuses on. So feed it positive, successful thoughts."
Debra W. Girlten

Q: Who do I want as friends?

"Mistakes are just steps on a journey to success."
Paul Roberts

Q: How could I build stronger relationships with people who are important to me?

"What we do is nothing but a drop in the ocean, but if we didn't do it, the ocean would be one drop less."
Mother Teresa

Q: Which aspect of my job do I value most?

"Write down your goals – the worst ink survives the best memory."
Harriett Gilbert

Q: Where do I want to go on holiday?

"You must be the change you wish to see in the world."
Mahatma Gandhi

Q: What is my ideal job?

"Things work out best for the people who make the best out of the way things turned out."
John Robert Wooden

Q: How much time do I want to spend with my family?

"Whether you think you can or you can't – you are right."
Henry Ford

48

Q: What do I want to do this weekend?

"Our aspirations are our possibilities."
Robert Browning

Q: What has prevented me in the past from making a difference?

"There is no security in life, only opportunity."
Mark Twain

50

Q: How much do I want to weigh?

"You can be the difference that makes the difference."
Gerrant Blewid

51

Q: What gives me hope?

"May you live all the days of your life."
Jonathan Swift

52

Q: Which places do I want to visit?

"The world's greatest thinkers were great because they translated their thoughts into action."
Ricky Muddimer

Q: What luxury item would I like to buy for myself?

"I dream for a living."
Steven Spielberg

Q: What dreams do I want to pursue?

"The future belongs to those who believe in the beauty of their dreams."
Eleanor Roosevelt

Q: What ruts do I want to escape from?

"If we did all the things we are capable of doing,
we would literally astound ourselves."
Thomas A. Edison

Q: What possibilities do I need to consider in order to make a difference in my life?

"Your goal should be just out of reach, but not out of sight."
Denis Waitley & Reni L. Witt

Q: What specifically do I want to do, have, learn or become?

"Success is a science;
if you have the conditions, you get the result."
Oscar Wilde

58

Q: Who could possibly help me?

"Be not afraid of going slowly, be only afraid of standing still."
Chinese Proverb

Q: What resources might I need?

"Nothing is more powerful than an idea whose time has come."
Victor Hugo

60

Q: What could I possibly do to increase my self-belief?

"You'll never discovery new oceans unless you have the courage to leave the shore."
Jo Hutchinson

Q: How could I possibly persuade others to help me make a difference?

"If it is to be, it is up to me."
Unknown

Q: What are my personal goals?

"Imagination is more powerful than knowledge, for knowledge is limited to all we know and understand, whilst imagination embraces the entire world, and all there ever will be to know and undertstand."
Albert Einstein

Q: What qualities do I most admire in others?

"The possibilities of creative effort connected with the subconscious mind are stupendous and imponderable. They inspire one with awe."
Napoleon Hill

Q: How will I measure my success?

"The best time to plant a tree was twenty years ago.
The second best time is now."
Chinese Proverb

Q: What do I aspire to?

"I will go anywhere as long as it is forward."
David Livingston

66

Q: What do I feel passionate about?

"Whistle while you work."
The Seven Dwarfs

Q: What single thing would make the greatest difference in my life?

"Making and keeping promises to ourselves precedes making promises and keeping promises to others."
Stephen R. Covey

Q: What makes me enthusiastic?

"It is not fair to ask of others what you are not willing to do yourself."
Eleanor Roosevelt

Q: What needs to happen next?

"We think too small. Like the frog at the bottom of the well. He thinks the sky is only as big as the top of the well. If he surfaced, he would have an entirely different view."
Mao Tse-Tung

Q: How confident am I?

"Never look down on anyone, unless you are helping them up."
Rev. Jesse Jackson

Q: How healthy is my lifestyle?

"It is the mark of good action that it appears inevitable in retrospect."
Robert Louis Stevenson

Q: What skills do I need to develop?

"Don't let what you cannot do interfere with what you can do."
John Robert Wooden

Q: What subject might I enjoy learning about?

"Failure is an event, not a person."
Zig Ziglar

74

Q: How well balanced is my life?

"Idleness is the holiday of fools."
G. K. Chesterton

Q: What financial goals do I have?

"The future belongs to those who prepare for it."
Ralph Waldo Emerson

Q: What do I want to become more confident about?

"What lies behind us and what lies before us are tiny matters compared with what lies within us."
Oliver Wendell Holmes

Q: What fitness goals do I have?

"You don't need to know anymore; you just need to apply more of what you already know."
N.L. Waterbridge

78

Q: What are the possible risks and implications of moving towards my goal?

"Why focus on growing old? Why not keep your mind active and vow to die young, as late as possible!"
Linda Bergwert

Q: What standards do I want to set for myself?

"It is useless to desire more time if
you are already wasting what little you have."
James Allen

Q: What inspires me?

"Even if you are on the right track,
you'll get run over if you just sit there."
Will Rogers

Q: How relaxed am I?

"The only way to find out the limits of the possible is by going beyond them into the impossible."
Arthur C. Clarke

Q: What do I want less of?

"It's not hard to make decisions when you know what your values are."
Roy Disney

Q: What do I want more of?

"The greatest thing in this world is not so much where we are, but in which direction we are moving."
Oliver Wendell Holmes

Q: Which direction am I moving in?

"No one is useless in this world who lightens the burden of another."
Charles Dickens

Q: How important is the environment?

"The minute you begin to do what you want to do,
it's really a different kind of life."
Buckminster Fuller

Q: What might I possibly contribute to others?

"If you can dream it, you can do it."
Walt Disney

Q: How much personal responsibility am I taking for my career development?

"Good intentions mean nothing if they remain inside you."
Gina L. Tredbrew

Q: Which personal qualities would I benefit from developing?

"If you don't jump, you won't land."
Unknown

89

Q: How many times do I complain about the weather?

"Happiness is a habit — cultivate it."
Elbert Hubbard

Q: What is the state of my social life?

"The key to happiness is having dreams.
The key to success is making dreams come true."
Unknown

Q: What promise will I make to myself?

"And the trouble is, if you don't risk anything, you risk even more."
Erica Long

Q: What do I contribute to my employer?

"The more doors you open the more you increase your probability of success."
Jules Agombar

Q: What could I say to keep myself going?

"I am still learning."
Michelangelo

Q: When did I last compliment myself?

"What one does is what counts and not what one had the intention of doing."
Pablo Picasso

Q: How could I possibly make a difference at work?

"Whatever the mind can conceive and believe, it can achieve."
Napoleon Hill

Q: How much do I like myself?

"The way I see it, if you want the rainbow,
you gotta put up with the rain."
Dolly Parton

Q: What leisure interests do I want to resume?

"A wise man creates more opportunities than he finds."
Francis Bacon

Q: How do I show others I love them?

"There is no such thing as a career path.
It is crazy paving and you have to lay it yourself."
Dominic Cadbury

Q: Who do I admire?

"The future belongs to people who see possibilities before they become obvious."
Theodore Leavitt

Q: What sort of property do I want to live in?

"It is never too late to be what you might have been."
George Eliot

101

Q: How much TV do I really need to watch?

"Always bear in mind that your own resolution to succeed is more important than any other one thing."
Abraham Lincoln

Q: How do I measure the success of my relationship?

"To succeed you have to believe in something with such a passion that it becomes reality."
Anita Roddick

Q: What could bring more fun into my life?

"It is our attitude at the beginning of a difficult undertaking
which more than anything else,
will determine its successful outcome."
William James

Q: Who do I want to work with?

"Quality is remembered long after the price is forgotten."
Gucci Family slogan

105

Q: What gives me that 'feel good' factor?

"Why focus on recalling past problems when you could be thinking of solutions to take you forward."
Rob Smith

Q: How many of my fears are imagined?

"Before anything else, getting ready is the secret of success."
Henry Ford

Q: What possibilities do I see?

"If I really want to improve my situation, I can work on the one thing over which I have control – myself."
Stephen R. Covey

Q: What do I want to learn to live with?

"If you wait until the wind and the weather are just right, you will never plant anything and never harvest anything."
Ecclesiastes 11:4

Q: What could possibly increase team spirit?

"Life is no brief candle, but a splendid torch."
George Bernard Shaw

Q: Which mental blocks do I want to overcome?

"Some men have thousands of reasons why they cannot do what they want to, when all they need is one reason they can."
Willis R. Whitney

III

Q: What do I want to be more tolerant of?

"Can we fix it? Yes we can!"
Bob the Builder

Q: How could I possibly help my partner?

"Life is either a daring adventure or nothing."
Helen Keller

Q: What would I love to celebrate?

"Without vision the people perish."
Proverbs 29:18

Q: What have I been procrastinating about?

"It is not the mountain we conquer, but ourselves."
Sir Edmund Hillary

Q: Am I moving towards something or away from something?

"One of the simplest things about all the facts of life is that to get where you want to go you must keep on keeping on."
Norman Vincent Peale

Q: What will ensure my success?

"It's either right or it's wrong and you'll know the difference."
Charlie Haggie

Q: How can I possibly reduce the level of pressure on myself?

"Life's most urgent question is, what are you doing for others?"
Martin Luther King, Jr.

Q: What does completion look like?

"We don't see things as they are, we see things as we are."
Anais Nin

Q: What is the quality of my closest relationship?

"A candle loses nothing by lighting another candle."
Unknown

Q: How could I possibly make more opportunities for myself?

"Success is for you, not others, to define."
Big Dan Trewler

Q: What is it most helpful for me to focus on in life?

"Life is full of endless possibilities."
Rosalyn Palmer

Q: What do I really want to achieve?

"In times of change the learners will inherit the earth, while the learned find themselves beautifully equipped to deal with a world that no longer exists."
Eric Hoffer

Q: What are my core values?

"I will not let anyone walk through my mind with their dirty feet."
Mahatma Gandhi

Q: What could I possibly do differently today?

"If you believe in yourself – you'll find it makes a difference!"
Suzanne Wood

125

Q: Which friend can I most easily help to make a difference?

If you would like to discover more about making a difference you might want to consider the following publications and learning resources produced by **Andy Gilbert** and the **Go MAD Thinking** team:

Discover more ways to Make A Difference

Our extensive resource and publications range is available from www.gomadthinking.com or telephone +44 (0)1509 891313 to place an order.

Multi-media resources

Thinking for Business Success
– Top ranking business and management podcast series on iTunes – download for free!

www.gomadthinking.tv
– An online resource library containing over 150 video, text and audio resources.

Books on business development

Go MAD – The art of making a difference
– The original Go MAD personal effectiveness book and a great introduction to the Go MAD® Thinking System.
(0-9543292-6-0)

Go MAD About Negotiating
– Negotiation – made easy! Achieving results through influencing the thinking of others. Practical easy-to-read case-studies and over 150 tips to consider when negotiating.
(0-9551287-0-6)

Contagious Customer Care
– Easy-to-read case-studies and practical tips about making a difference.
(0-9537284-5-5)

Books on coaching

Go MAD About Coaching + audio CD (via voucher)
– Over 200 powerful coaching questions, plus tips, tools, techniques and templates. The manager's guide for helping others to make a difference.
(0-9537284-8-X)

Books on personal development

Who's driving your bus?
– An inspirational story about the power of the Go MAD® Thinking System.
(0-9537284-9-8)

59 Minutes to a Calmer Life
– Practical strategies to help reduce stress in your professional and personal life.
(0-9537284-3-9)

Brain Magic
– The secrets to living a longer, happier and healthier life are within your grasp!
(0-9543292-8-7)

How to guides

How to Save Time and Money By Managing Meetings Effectively
– 101 ways to lead meetings that create clearly defined outputs and engage people.
(0-9543292-2-8)

How to Save Time and Money By Managing Organisational Change Effectively
– Essential tools to unlock the secrets of change and achieve effective transition.
(0-9543292-1-X)

How to Make A Difference By Transforming Managers into Leaders
– 255 thought provoking tips to create passionate leaders who make a difference and love what they do.
(0-9543292-3-6)

How to win in negotiations
– 130 tips for any one to adopt immediately in any negotiation to make a difference.
(0-9543292-5-2)

How to avoid the training trap
– 101 ways to ensure that development gives a great return on investment and really Makes A Difference.
(0-9551287-3-0)

How to create a culture of commitment in your contact centre
– 101 tips that will make your contact centre a great place to work.
(0-9551287-4-9)

Audio

Brain Magic 6 CD audio pack
– The secrets to living a longer, happier and healthier life are within your grasp!
(0-9543292-4-4)

There's Always a Deal 6 CD audio pack
– Learn how to prepare for and conduct successful negotiations.
(0-9551287-2-1)

Taking presentation skills to a new level
Your Questions Answered CD 1
– Discover how to make more powerful, professional and memorable presentations.
(0-9543292-7-9)

Dealing effectively with difficult people
Your Questions Answered CD 2
– Discover how to understand difficult people and improve their performance at work.
(0-9543292-7-9)

Obtaining profitable referrals
Your Questions Answered CD 3
– Discover how to obtain profitable referrals from existing customers.
(0-9543292-7-9)

Increasing sales results
Your Questions Answered CD 4
– Discover how to apply powerful techniques at each stage of the sales process.
(0-9543292-7-9)

Achieving business success through powerful design & marketing
Your Questions Answered CD 5
– Discover how to design powerful print and web based marketing materials.
(0-9543292-7-9)

Building high trust, sustainable relationships
Your Questions Answered CD 6
– Discover how to build high trust, sustainable relationships with high level customers.
(0-9543292-7-9)

Business improvement through transformed thinking
Your Questions Answered CD 7
– Discover how to improve business performance through the development of people's thinking ability.
(0-9543292-7-9)

Learn the secrets of successful property investors
Your Questions Answered CD 8
– Discover how to safely invest in property to minimise your risk and maximise your return.
(0-9543292-7-9)

Negotiating for results –
Your Questions Answered CD 9
– Discover how everyone can negotiate, and every negotiator can improve.
(0-9543292-7-9)

Ebooks

Available to download from www.gomadthinking.com

How to achieve what you want, when you want!
– Seven powerful principles of successful thinking for work, life and everything.

How to develop a personal passion
– Practical tips and insights to increase your motivation to achieve.

How to determine what you want and when you want it
– Pragmatic steps to leaping into the top five percent of goal definers.

How to produce plentiful possibilities, pressing priorities and perfect plans
– Quick and easy tips to plan success, eliminate time wasting and get started.

How to create a self-belief that you can and will achieve
– Powerful insights into building the confidence to succeed.

How to get others on your side
– Definitive guidelines on involving others and getting them on your side to achieve what you want.

How to make personal choices and take responsibility
– Insightful ideas to help you own your thoughts and actions and increase your probability of success.

How to guarantee your success
– Clear and simple advice on challenging your thinking and tips on taking actions and measuring results.

Making a difference workbook
– 30 activities and exercises for successful thinking about work, life and everything.

You can purchase a full set of How to ebooks (including Making A Difference workbook) for a complete guide to making a difference to work, life and everything.

Go to work on your career
– Practical tips, tools and techniques for developing your career. Including case-studies and numerous exercises, this book is a must read for anyone wanting to make a difference to their career.

Why not sign up to our regular free ezine and receive a free ebook? Subscribe via www.gomadthinking.com.

Telephone orders taken on +44(0)1509 891313.

Applying Go MAD Thinking with organisations

If you are seeking to make a difference within your organisation and would like to have a discussion about any aspect of applying Go MAD as a solution focused approach to leadership thinking, business improvement, coaching, management development or cultural change, then please contact us and a Go MAD Thinking Engineer will be happy to discuss possibilities.